Muscle and Blame

by
Des Dillon

Copyright © 2021

All rights reserved. No part of this publication may be reproduced, stored, or placed into a retrieval system, or transmitted in any form, or by any means, whether electronic, mechanical, photocopying, recording or otherwise, without the publisher's prior written consent.

This book is sold subject to the condition that it shall not in any way, be lent, resold, hired out, or otherwise circulated without the prior written consent of the publisher, in any form of binding or cover other than that in which it is published.

The moral rights of the author have been asserted in accordance with the Copyright, Designs and Patents Act 1988

Published by Second Sands Publications 2021
18 North Main Street,
Wigtown.
DG8 9HL

ISBN 978 0 9926576 3 5

Edited by Gillian Hamnett of Dark Sky Pages
Typeset in Bembo Std
Printed and bound by JB Print

Poems and artwork
by Des Dillon

This book is dedicated to
Billy McGowan and his budgie

Contents

Family
Daily bread	11
Though soft you tread above	12
I call your names in the old house	13
The universe watches	15
I am looking for unbreathed air	16
She placed eight pebbles	17
David's wake	18
Aurora	19
Lena Zavaroni	20
The boy	21
How to spell Junkie	22

Death
The white construction cranes	27
Covid	28
Lorelei	29
Five a.m.	30
You walked in colour	31
Make me music	32
What went before	33
I am not entirely convinced by salt	34
There's no telling what a lonely man might do	35
The suicide of Michelangelo Prufrock	36
Lighting	37

Philosophy
Things to learn from a spoon	41
Where we sit	42
Christmas poem	43
What the chair says	45
Bar-L ballad	46

Nature
Assuming the absence of bells	49
The rescue dog	50
Solar eclipse	51
A hand span below the heart	52
The numbers of the night	53
Element	54
Twa dugz	55
Snowman	56
The final berries (for John McMahon)	57
Manna	59
Mud dolphins	60
McGonnigle hates crows	61

Love
Resurrection	65
The force that pushes blossoms	66
Measures	67
Avocado	68
Savoy Centre	69
Never gonna dance	70

Reflections #3	71
Morning	72
Put the touchscreen down	73
Survivor	74
Body	75

Politics

Equivalent VIII	79
Babushka in Lybidska	80
Celtic wedding ring	82
Wedding #1 The Meal	84
Wedding #2 The Dance	85
Wedding #3 The Party	86
Wedding #4 The Parting Glass	87
Garden of Remembrance, Falls Road	88
Outside of Kilmainham	89
How to spell Nationalist	90
The Tory	91
On est tous des sauvages	92
Fuadach nan Gàidheal	93
Arc de Triomphe	94
American sweetheart	95
Gordonstoun School	96
Body politic	97
Uprising	98
Shipping	99
How to spell Ned	100
Publication credits and poem notes	*102*

Family

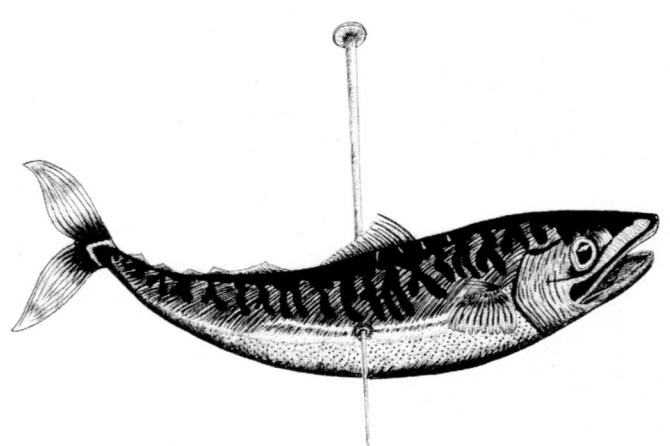

Daily bread

He fried eleven fish, fed us and said
Eat, I've knocked my fuckin pan in for this.
But my altar boy ears heard
Take this all of you
and eat it. This is my body
which will be given up for you daily
in white hot steelworks and wet construction sites.
His hands drove nails through the toughest timbers.
His sides bled sweat and blistered vinegar.

Yet, throughout the last days, we had him wear
a crown of thorns because he drank cheap wine
day and night to escape our spears and slings
over things that went not quite right for us.
Thankless children, muscle work, alcohol and blame?
The end was always going to be the same.

Though soft you tread above

I opened my mouth
and my mother's voice came out.
And she did hear
though soft she tread above me.

And I have spoken
with my father's voice
against the sweet flute-like notes
on the snow-filled floor
and I had thought
to speak no more.

I call your names in the old house

Derelict, awaiting demolition,
five bedrooms crouching;
I call your names in the night,
Caroline! Linda! Angie!
My voice and echo silenced, then
a swinging door says
The things you look for are dead.
Can't you smell damp plaster
falling from the walls?
I walk onto thinly lit streets –
Stevie! Geraldine! Wendy!
Names burrowing down the lane
and fifty years of heartbreak.
I shout to where the swing park used to be –
David! Donna! Anybody?
I'm the last one of the family.
The past is built on grief and love
and tomorrow comes with thunderous trucks.

The universe watches

I still remember that salmon
resplendent with recent death,
the sun on scales of stainless steel,
the bloody priest that dents its head.

An imagined last twitch of the tail
though his eyes were bubbles.
It didn't feel right, my father's smile
and me with the priest in my fist.

A bitterness hovered
over the loch-side fire.
The flesh salted with regret.
And far above the blurry mountains,
starry pinpoint eyes of guilt.

I am looking for unbreathed air

I am looking for unbreathed air,
water never touched before,
the ground unstepped upon,
the lick of flame that doesn't burn.
They say life is too short;
I say it's far too long.
I'm fed up already
and I'm only fifty-one.
I've met each person so many times,
I could pre-empt and say their lines.
There must be something, somewhere,
to stop me marking out my time.
When I was ten I filled three jars:
one with acid steel town air,
one with yellow water from the pond,
the third with lumps of iron ore.
I can't say why I did this.
I can't say what it means.
But one day soon I'll burst the seals
and rent apart the seams.

She placed eight pebbles

She placed eight pebbles
between her toes,
waddled and
sunk
her feet
through clear water into sand.
I remember nothing else of that day
except one by one
we threw them at the sun.

Many tides have separated us.

It would be easier now
to find those pebbles
than that day.

My mother's song was
The water is deep.
With this body I can't swim over
but when the time has come
I'll drop it from me
and fly like a bird to the sun.

David's wake

We slept on his floor on a blow-up bed,
right where they found him dying with the drink.
Mad cunts in the close kept us up all night
with singing and fighting shenanigans
yet chucked in thirty-four quid for a wreath.
Alfie, three months sober, went round the doors.
They're no bad cunts Dessie, he said, just the drink.

He pinned a note to the drying room door
of the neighbours' grief on David's passing.
The receipt was taped and highlighted pink:
Proof of purchase.
Proof of sobriety.
No one should judge but why am I surprised
that Alfie is good with apostrophes?

Aurora

When my mother carried me out to see
the Northern Lights, her hair smelled of stars
and her arms were white as the Milky Way.
That night, innocence was in me. Some days,
cynical, I would call this nostalgia.
Today I'm thinking of that innocence
as the glowing umbilical cord to
pre-conception – the free bliss of being.

Mother, the glint and echo of diamonds
in your hair and old lines now pave the way:
I've been a wanderer all of my days
and many a sight have I seen.
Sing me now,
beyond the heavenly dancers,
to obliteration in the universe.

Lena Zavaroni

Tonight's ferry floats upon her ghost;
the Zavaroni chip-shop sign summons
up the 70s. Maybe the words were red,
but they're tired now and tilted slightly.
Traces of chips and vinegar drag me
to flared-trousered lunch-time first-year love,
radio belting out *Mama he's makin' eyes at me*
and I'm imagining Angie Maguire singing
even though her mother was dead and she
was nearly an orphan except for her dad
who found me Bay-City-Roller drunk
in her garden and phoned the stomach pump.
And wine's promises are a curse like fame,
Lena, thinning away like the chip-shop sign.

The boy

This boy, he looks like my brother.
His hair is blonde, his freckles fair,
his ears and nose stick out to there.

Without being obvious I watch him turn
and sure enough, his nose is a boat.
I give him more leeway than the other kids
even though he's cheeky as fuck,
and watch
my brother's arrogant vulnerability
come down the years.
And lighted by the sun,
the pink enchantment of his ears.

They say the dead shall not return.

Yet here he is, framed and backlit
by a west facing window of a Stranraer school:

a whole new future, paved with woe
I thole him till it's time to go.

How to spell Junkie

J is for Johnny and the jailer
who let him out early
one blue morning from Barlinnie.

U is for up at Asda's, crack of dawn
where Angie went to buy her son
his favourite things for coming home.

N is no one knows
why he left her house
for a darkened close.

(N is for needle
and overdose.)

And I never knew that
K is minus two hundred
and seventy-three degrees Kelvin,
so cold, nothing in the cosmos moves.
But that's where Angie went
when she heard the news.

And now

I is for all the ifs and painful onlys
that Angie carries ever lonely.
And E?

I heard her say
beside the grave
when the priest was done,
'Everybody's someone's daughter.
Everybody's someone's son.'

Death

The white construction cranes

So much depends upon the trinity of cranes
washed with violet light on the Glasgow skyline.
They watch over me, blinking and nodding,
framed by my hotel window.
The tall cranes have listened
and I have spoken my troubles to them.
I have prayed nine nights
to my tall companions.
If I die before I wake
I pray the cranes my soul to take.
And if I wake today again
I hope they're watching,
glazed with rain.

Covid

Even my shadow is wrinkled with wear
and the sun has done no good.
It makes me cough
like the hunchback
who lived where I was young.
He is moving through the wheat
like a giant crow;
his cough the target
for the stones we throw.

Lorelei

The Solway's molten aluminium
hypnotic swells of surface sunlight
and ionised tang awakes a torment
down deep blue tides in my blood. Lorelei
and Serein lullaby my DNA
through cold fathoms of evolution.
I remember the tsunami. A man
on the shore staring at miles of ocean

floor in silence as bathers ran in fear.
When the sea thundered back on white horses
this man held perfect peace till impact.
And now that I'm sure what his stillness meant,
I flip headfirst into the divine chill,
sinking towards truth through filtered rays of sun.

Five a.m.

Glasgow never really slept last night,
She just wound down to pauses of silence
drunken shouts and the squeal of bus brakes.
Then the big engines of the morning roar,
searching out the first footfalls of dawn
to sweep them up and carry them on.
Without meaning or hope or purpose to life,
we accelerate hard away from the light.

A toilet flushes, then another. The clink
of cups, rushing showers, clip of doors.
People brushing along the corridors.
Some to breakfast, some to cars, and some
to early morning bars. I long to dress
and like a feather on a breeze, blow past.

You walked in colour

The freshly hung clothes
drip teardrops for the days
you wore them in the sun.
You walked in colour
down our summers
waving a blade of grass:
it whispers still.

The clothes creased and flapped
and clung to your thighs with the breeze,
your nipples pointing forward,
underwear impregnated with your scents.
Now the washing cries blacks and blues
to the fading colours of those days.
My sister washed your clothes today,
as if the past can fold away.

Make me music

Therefore, knit my veins
and arteries
to make a players seat.
Fashion plectrums
from my nails,
four drums from my skin.
String my sinews on my skull
and fiddle my lament.
Turn my bones to xylophones.
Knit a robin's nest of my hair –
place it in my pelvic bone
where he can sing alone.
And throw the rest
to the gulls' opera on the wall.
On this one last song
my soul will rise or fall.

What went before

Take me through the hearts of soaring birds,
the cold and tiny pump of darting fish,
the pulse and sweep of anemones
to the first blip of life.
Then onto death without shore,
the space after the first swelling beat
of the universe.
We all know what happened next.
I need to hear what went before.

I am not entirely convinced by salt

Your bitterness kisses my lips with the lips of the sea.
My tongue recoils at sudden grit and holiness.
Saliva pours forth for a taste.
And though you dissolve into me,
when I emerge into summer heat
you glitter me from forehead to feet.
Even when you sparkle in the sun,
I am not convinced.
Your whites and reds and purple pinks
do nothing more than make me think
I am not entirely convinced by salt.
You rattle and hiss when you pour,
ward off evil, shoulder to the floor,
preserve, heal wounds and more.
I am not convinced entirely by salt,
yet you have made your way to my heart
and when I fly my dusted soul
away from skin, may it crystalise a star.

There's no telling what a lonely man might do

There's no telling what a lonely man might do:
Visit you twice a week until midnight.
Say he doesn't want tea
then talk food all night long.
Drive the dark roads till the sun comes up.
Or buy a rope to soothe his pain,
knowing the possibility is always there.
Sit by the beach wondering if trees have elbows,
if waves can hear their own whispers,
if the white heron on the rock dreams of love?

The suicide of Michelangelo Prufrock

I measured out my life with Facebook likes.
Selfies weighing flows and ebbs of self-esteem,
I paint a world – a pixelated dream.
Building a life by album posts and lists –
comments and pokes and provokes and evokes,
and shares are there so therefore I exist.
On the sidebar, cold friends light green and go,
mourning the death of Michelangelo.

'your an angel. RIP.' Fill my wall.
each desperate electronic wail
a misspelled need to real-connect us all?
This widescreen silent tombstone flickers on,
status unchanged, password unknown: a face,
a half-naked smiling ghost lost in cyberspace.

Lighting

This streetlight is a heron looking for fish
in the pool of its own light.

This one a mother searching for her child
who has stepped into the darkness.

This one an old man with a bad neck
looking for where his life has gone.

And this one, at the crossroads, a priest
praying over a coffin, rosary beads swinging.

Philosophy

Things to learn from a spoon

Concave, convex. Angle of incidence equals angle of reflection.
Design, refraction, reflection.
Iron ore and smelting.
Stainless steel, coffee, sugar.
T. S. Eliot and measure.
The hydrodynamics of tea.
Heat conduction.
Spoonerisms. Beauty.
Turning faces upside down.
Worlds inside out.
Rhythm, the music of spoons.
An industry of spoons.
Moulding, scalding.
Silver spoons, entitled mouths.
Spooning, silver plate.
Nickel, all kinds of metal.
The periodic table.
Setting tables, etiquette.
Things undiscovered yet.
The love of two cups of tea.
To hang your spoon upon a tree
to puzzle birds and mice.
And finally: they're nice.

Where we sit

This little red-haired girl
has been playing
in the sand
since we paddled
into Jumbile Bayou.
She has made a world
just where she sits,
and I have learned from that.

Christmas poem

Walking frosted fields,
each crunching footfall sounds
like horses galloping
the bounds of knowledge.

And if Kant and Schopenhauer
are right, I move in a world
I know nothing about.
And beneath my feet
Christmas horses
thunder into Bethlehem.

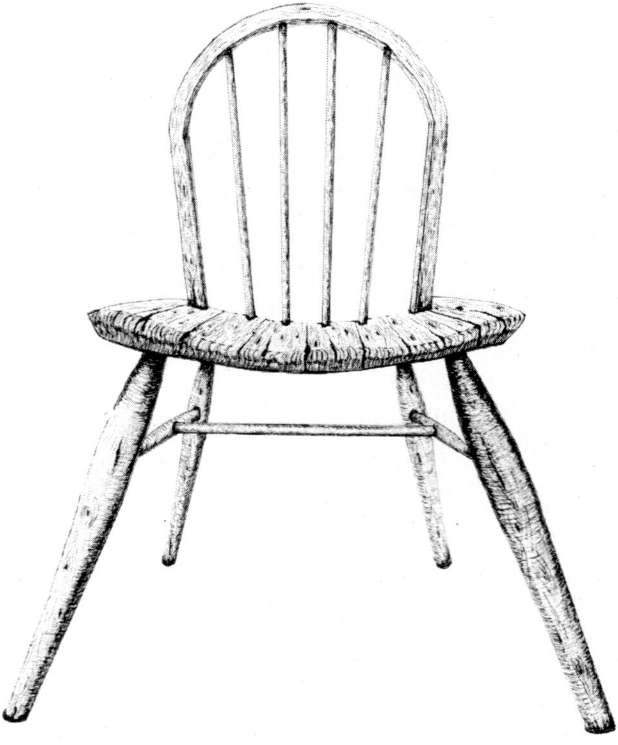

What the chair says

Every object has its word or meaning
to convey. The empty chair in the garden
doesn't say chair at all. It stares
a pressure at me, a silent watcher while
the actual chair chops and filters the wind:
its real meaning steady and profound.
My years with this chair have unlocked
the eucalyptus rattle, the monkey puzzle's

waving arms. The trembling cherry, swing
seat, blackbird's eye, film
reel of the sky, the smell of new
turned earth, frost and sun.
It takes courage to sit in that chair
and whatever is there, takes me everywhere.

Bar-L ballad

The ghost of A hall sings to midnight cells.
I wanna go home I wanna go home
to ma wee hoose in Barlinnie.
Our powder plunges chilly nights into
weeks till years and wives and kids fall away.
The porridge is great, ye don't need a plate
ye only need a hammer an a chisel.
Spirit, meet me naked in my sleep.

Shred these prison clothes and sheets.
Smash skin, sinew and muscle. Toss
my guilt-ridden bones clattering up
the landing. Wire what's left to the stars
so that I'm a tiny thing, pleading before
that which watches and never once blinks.

Nature

Assuming the absence of bells

I will measure time
by the kisses of dogs,
their claws clicking
on the old church road.
Stabs of wild garlic punch out white flowers.
Swallows arrive,
light on mint and daisies,
Swallows depart,
brown leaves bursting in my hands,
snow on the flats of my feet.
I refuse to measure weeks.
Days will be sunlight on grass,
shadows fall and rise
with the purple tilting of the skies.
Nights will be peatbog fires,
grumbling packs of dogs
measuring my dreams.
And dawn will be welcomed
like the birth that's never tolled,
assuming the absence of bells.

The rescue dog

Scout swallowed Ruby's snaps and growls and barked
them out as play. They're curled exhausted now
like the silence after the kettle has
clicked. I settle to a full bright focus
on the window-ledge plant vibrating green.
I don't know its name but still imagine
it might secrete a certain chemical
cure for mortal illness or infection.

God winks, for every sin's a hidden cure.
The quiet in the universe before
the Big Bang made one quivering diamond
dot of perfect sense. Passing a jot
of sense into all things – medicine. Twa dugs –
one vicious, one calm – sleep together, Ying and
Yang.

Solar eclipse

Chattering sparrows croaking crows pigeons
cooing. The roar of a bus. Cherry trees
rustle. A child shouts. Waves break on sand.
The child wails. A front door slams.
Cock a doodle doo. A Facebook ping.
An umbrella of birds chirp and answer, crow
to crow, dove to dove. Blackbirds alarm
their babies. Farm machinery dies away

into silence. Which is cut apart
by a chain of strangely howling dogs
fading to the creak of greenhouse glass cooled
as the moon drags her darkness over the sun.
I open my eyes into awful dusk and such
silence as to feel the gasp of the world in my chest.

A hand span below the heart

I press my face to the night sky.
I don't just look up,
I actually *press* my face
so that I am,
in some way,
connected with
the other end of the universe,
the mystery of distance.

And it answers me,
not from out there,
but from a hand span
below the heart.

I have travelled all
of time and space
to find a God
where I press my face.

The numbers of the night

The numbers of the night
cannot be counted,
no matter what they say.
They can be seen and felt,
the Milky Way a pelt
pulled over the cold nightfall.
The stars' binary chatter
to other stars behind and further.
And yet we try to discover,
like an ant could fathom
the whole ocean
from a salty drop of the sea
on the warm we-t bark of a cherry tree.
I am a man out to discover
the numbering of the numbers.
And even though I know
the numbers cannot be counted,
I carry on in the faith
that something will be found,
undaunted.

Element

Night's hoods of silence
send wind back, settled to her box.
Aeolis, Aeolis I whisper, but nothing.
I'm sure the stars roar their nuclear furnace,
yet from this distance they blink
like raindrops on tar – a tiny half-imagined sound.
The sea is on pause at the turn of the tide
and the creatures wait, fully aware –
in the moment – of their existence.
God's within the undisturbed stillness, I'm sure.
The stars flaked on black water,
the wondrous eyes of fish and creatures.
The trees and their dark reflection,
are the silence as I am too.
I wasn't born screaming into chaos
but before; before the desperate journey
of the sperm, to the ecstasy of the egg.
I was born from this element of silence,
waiting in sea and tree and rock
and standing behind,
breathing on my neck.

Twa dugz

The cows kiss Bailey only when he's epileptic.
They follow him like a God running along fences
and when he stops,
they rasp his head with hairy tongues,
pushing and jostling to get next to him.
Maybe he gives off chemicals or brain waves,
or perhaps it is something much more wonderful.
But today love is the currency of the morning.
And I remember Kiev, the packs like wolves inured

to their old enemy padding past marching
rows of military policemen without a blink,
spring shadows of soldier and dog slanting
away. They came to me out of the blinding sun
flowing around a moving tram through dust.
Kerbside kisses were the currency of that morning.

Snowman

In the middle of the mountain pass,
leaving the radio on against the dark,
I step out for a piss.
The priests sing Silent Night
into this black cathedral.
And as I piss, head tilted to the sky,
snowflakes floating down in silver millions,
warm on my lips, cold on my eye,
I stand in a cloud of steam
receiving angels till I am clean
and white.
In the headlights all is calm,
all is bright.
Sleep in heavenly peace.
I stand upon a precipice.

The final berries (for John McMahon)

I fear that God's been shunted from his place,
and these trillion scattered pin lights of stars
murmur only to the vacuum of space.
No one hears the comets' whispering light,
trundling planets singing opera to the sun,
or sees that gasping yellow face on the moon.
My soul amplifies the grunts of thunderclouds
and spinning birds' frantic arpeggios.

The dolphin leaps to hear the commotion
and her splash glugs the news to startled fish:
that my beehive's quiet honeycomb asks
where have all the bees gone? The still roses
tilt skywards for answers but the red lips
of the winter berries have kissed the snow.

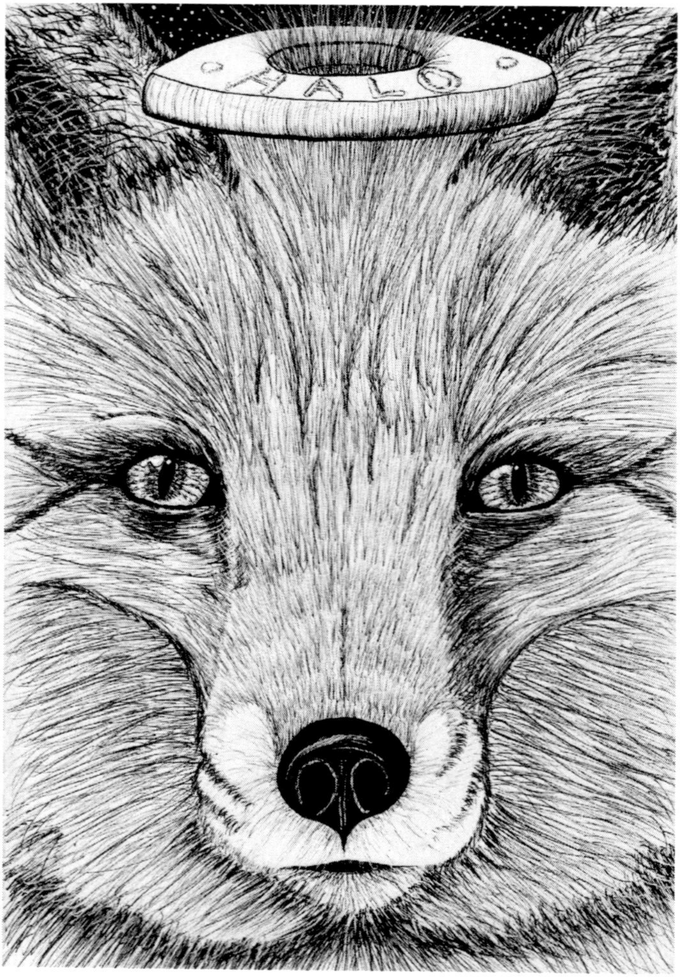
HALO

Manna

On a snowbound single-track mountain road:
a fox. Her frosted coat a drift of stars.
I crunched to a halt. *The fuck're ye doing
on the road?* The universe floated
in her eyes. *Do ye want a wee sweetie?*
Hungry she said, by a bow of her head.
Dropping it on snow a foot from the car,
I swapped the fox a polo mint for trust.

She looked at me. The mint. Me.
Licked. Blinked. Picked
and backed into pine behind fogs of breath.
In dusts of snow five bright cubs appeared.
I scattered a packet of minty manna.
And coming home – six kebabs in heather.

Mud dolphins

These pigs, these dolphins of the mud
snorters and bloaters and grubbers
as they hurry through the slurry
for food that floats and food that's buried –
their hard and hairy hides
our smoky bacon on the side.

And underneath his floppy ears,
his glassy clever holy eyes,
and in our kitchens every day
he fries fries fries.

McGonnigle hates crows

On the hot harbour wall a thousand crows
sweat and croon shoulder to shoulder under
a wilting sun like sailors home from the sea,
staggering on heavy land legs to the Anchor.
The crows know it's safer here than the woods –
far, far from the sport of McGonnigle's gun.
And here the cunt comes now angry as fuck,
like one hawthorn stick's a match for a murder.

They lure him away down to the turning tide,
swinging his stick in the quicksand banks,
flapping off when the sea pours over his boots.
Inside the frill of seaweed crisping in the sun
clicking sandflies calculate, one by one,
the days he'll burn in hell for the man that he's
become.

Love

Resurrection

My soul has been borrowed
from the Great Face in the Sky.
It will return imprinted
with the things that I've done.
Blemished with love,
limping hopelessly,
streaked with the long hours of the night –
it will give up the fight,
and like a balloon in a hurricane –
rise to search for you
among incandescent lights,
enter the mouths of stars
until my stains
are bleached
by their light.
When I find you
we will be Christ-Immaculate
and doubly married,
till life do us part.

The force that pushes blossoms

The force that pushes blossoms
from the cherry trees in spring,
or draws the crocus
from its frozen bulb,
will grind the sorrow out of me.

Pull flowers, doves and dragonflies
from the magician's starry hood.
Sculpt eggs in the bellies of birds.
Giant windmills of light
to roll the summer out.

But for now, whales call from the deep.
Wind tears at cornerstones
and the rain nails down the slates.
I keep watch
where the cherry blossoms will appear
in hope we make it through the year.

Measures

Our shadows are on the sea
with length and breadth
but no thickness.
Now there's a puzzle!
That love can have length and breadth,
but no thickness.

The ripples on water.
The light of the sun.
The breeze on our skin.
Yet a thinness thinner
than even one molecule
atom
electron
lepton
nothing.

Avocado

You made yourself a womb
and rebirthed me clean
from all the things of life.
I pushed myself in beads of blood
into the volume of your lungs.
You held your breath
till I was built
then exhaled me into
the moonlight of your eyes.
My skin peeled
and fell away.
I am avocado
revealing flesh
blessed by life's oil
which tastes of all the things
that taste of you.

Savoy Centre

Her breakfast is cheap tea and sausages,
licking bitter ketchup from her fingers.
This girl of old abandoned dreams shivers
at her Christmas stall – pretty, say thirty –
flirty half-smile stilled beneath a tinsel hat,
searches fingers and face for wedding marks.
But truth is a look and a nod from me
dissolving her smile and turning away.

Life's ice has sucked her lungs of hope
that a tall shining messiah would come
and she would be his own sweet religion,
forever and ever amen. Poor gift
I give. If she cries, then surely she'll sing
acapella – the torment of the thing.

Never gonna dance

You say I've never danced with you cos sober
feet ain't got no rhythm. But listen, you don't
only dance with your feet on the dance floor.
I've been dancing sean-nos unnoticed
through sickness and health, heel and toe over
these few square feet of Scotland. Unseen,
I have stamped out reels and jigs, shuffled
airs and laments over old friends gone,

floated through unbearable joy, spun
and tip-tapped in the garden through swallows
and blackbirds, howling dogs in the flowers,
cats' choirs in shivering cherry blossoms.
I have danced, darling. And I'm never
gonna dance again, the way I've danced with you.

Reflections #3

This frosted nest:
its iced beauty
has chilled the chirps of birds,
frozen the flutter of spring.

Winter creaks its way
around the house.
Your shoes are the frozen
ends of memories
threading my days
like the white
glittering straws
of the nest.

Morning

Everything in this garden knows your walk.
The dogs look up.
The birds look up.
The grass looks up.
The pond fish pull to you, their compass –
metal skin shedding golden water.
The gulls chuck down a friendly laugh
from the squint chimney pots.
The cherry blossoms twist like antennae,
deciphering you.
The mice come out of hiding,
hands cupping twitching noses,
hollering to the soaring
black weight of the raven
that you are here at last.

Put the touchscreen down

Touch – the flower trembles.
Tap twice – dusts of pollen.
Slide – the squeaky green of the long stem.
Pinch and spread – your nose falls down inside.

Touch – the water, ripples go worldwide.
Tap twice – humpback whales appear.
Slide – the water burbles and settles.
Pinch and spread – to eye a peering fish.

Touch – the moon for silver skin.
Tap twice – she'll roll her dark side down.
Slide – for shooting stars.
Drag and drop a Venus in your heart.

Touch me – I tremble.
Tap twice – my eyes blink open.
Slide – the hairs lift on my skin.
Pinch and spread – the lips of my mouth.
Drag and drop the universe on my tongue.

Survivor

On hot rocks unwashed by the tide, pom poms
of sea pinks slump under the humid sky
spreading this terrible emulsion, bleaching
towards autumn and one year since your death.
I gave you surface when you needed depth;
Scotland bit my tongue. Now what grief has gone
leaves space refilled by dread. Pour ashore haar,
sarcophagus-me between sky and sea.

I still sniff perfumed movies from your clothes,
our days remembered by my nose. I see
the times my mouth was stuffed with ice and eyes
as dead as glass; I could have spoken heart
and gut but managed only farce. For that
I clatter forever over the bones.

Body

Your shoulder tastes of sea salt
and southern winds.
The back of your neck
has a trace of old loved dogs.
Your lips taste of Easter snow,
melted by your tongue.
The warm flicker
of log-fire kisses your breasts.
A cool spring morning
is the perfume of your belly,
and between your legs
an ocean
filled with tingling stars.

Politics

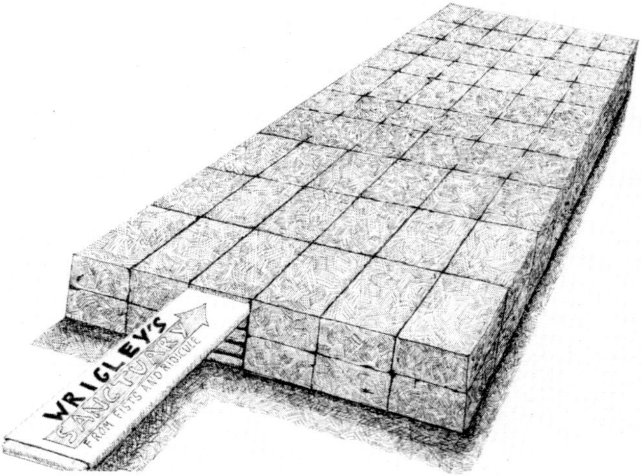
WRIGLEY'S
SANCTUARY
FROM FISTS AND RIDICULE

Equivalent VIII Culture War

When I was young and the Tate Gallery
bought that pile of bricks, I kept to myself
two secrets:
One — I liked those bricks and two —
why I liked those bricks.
I screwed Cola Joe's ice cream van
and amongst the Mint Cracknels,
Fizzy Lizzys, MB bars and Aztecs —
an intact pack of Wrigley's Spearmint Gum:
neat, pristine, cellophane wrapped rectangle's
definite edges soothing the sudden chaos
of hard drinking fathers with fists of steel.
My first secret hid from their ridicule.
I slid the other under my mattress,
that packet planked with spunked socks and porn
until the need for edges overwhelmed.

Babushka in Lybidska

She's stuck at the top of the insanely fast

dangerously
        steep
                escalator.

Babushka, born before The Terror,
living thirty years beyond her time,
gapes down into chaos. Her shawl stretches
around her body's history, a knot of busted
knuckles grip two sticks in one hand,
the fingers becoming the birch and trembling
in a makeshift A frame to the floor.
Metro workers push. She smells the rushing
flow of steel. Another hundred years
of perestroika will not get her there.
Put a man in front so she doesn't tumble!
But other sputniks in a hurry spit:
She ain't my mother! She ain't nobody's mother!
Babushka's right foot hovers over
the escalator.
Push her aside, we must move on!

Kyiv

    pours

        past .

Between the platform and the train
a blonde girl's foot pauses

        over the abyss

she will hover over when beauty has gone.
She hears the clatter of sticks and feels the weight
of the heavy body that falls within us all.

Celtic wedding ring

'Scots steel tempered wi' Irish fire
Is the weapon that I desire.'
~ Hugh MacDiarmid

With this ring I wed intimacy and solitude.
Two threads soldering
infinity with tears of gold.
I thanked God, in his still
and silent place, for you.
But my self had never come to rest
in a Scotland torn by religion
and London's tendons deep
in landscapes, oil, blood and laughing sheep.
I marched with Irish brio, hurling
and re-hurling prejudice and abuse
from clouds of Catholicism
onto concrete Calvinism:
two parallel hymns of separation
singing keyless in this Celtic nation.

In the Galloway ceilidh house
an Irish fire burns and the sweet
scented peat smoke twists
into the blue evening.

My hound races over wet sand.
He is two hounds mirrored,
feet never missing each other,
so fast the old ocean highways blur.
Foam and breeze whisper –
Fàilte Dhachaidh – welcome home.
This, the singular truth in John Doherty's fiddle
and being years before my final bed –
unpredicted and surprising – Scotland,
with this ring, and heart, and head
and everyone who bides here; I thee wed.

Wedding #1 The Meal

The bride, in white and curls falling, and the groom,
a smile to charm nuns and bankers, are seated.
In the craic, colourful hats and clamour, starters
are laid and I see a hundred Irelands on the plates.
In a green sea of calm jelly, Eire
presents its fragile alter of dreadful peace:
a slice of Orange laid there – out of place,
accepted as part yet not part – bittersweet

where would we be without it? On the Orange
a Red Hand of Ulster strawberry ironically unaware,
of its Sacred Heart possibilities. Radiant spirit.
Golden waves of melon lap the plate:
winding shores of Tír na nÓg where tides
rise over terror and float us all ashore.

Wedding #2 The Dance

She's the Queen of all things Irish.
A white-topped wave skirting shores
where ages and generations clap and sway
but things beneath and deep remain the same.
Irish Jive! She's this way, he's that, holding
the beat of one-two-three-spin –
holy trinity; hands in sacred grip.
Everybody join in! One-two-three-spin.

Later, in red, from the top table she watches
the little Irish dancers padding softly
over a heavy tradition of love and guns.
We've travelled far and weary us Irish.
On this Holy day, no one's thinking
of the dry-eyed bigot in the corner drinking.

Wedding #3 The Party

Four tall girls dance near the stage edge.
It could be the world's edge; the final precipice.
Or they could be four green future fields.
You'll be alright, alright. Like the complicated Celtic
circles embroidered on the breast of your dresses
you'll burst
from this dance floor through reels and jigs
and shining eyes.
Out and out and conquer far lands,
space even, because that girl is jumping heights

that leave us gasping at our own ability to leave
potato and bog and swing along on a song,
on the right road or the wrong, toward the stars'.
What is the stars? I ask Joxer, *What is the stars?*
That is the question. And what is the moon too?
And this wedding – what does it mean? What does it do?

Wedding #4 The Parting Glass

We've come to Marion's wedding from prison ships,
universities, armalites, Carmelite abbeys and schemes,
the shuffling diaspora of migration and famine and
fear.
Always moving out, pushing up.
On building sites and mines, motorways and roads,
steelworks, railways and drunken jail cells, corners
in asylums, parks, ghettos and slums. We sang
our songs till the walls were damp with tears.

Now our children and our children's children
Will climb the steps we've built for them
with poems and tears and laughter and guns.
May they always, always sing our songs.
In the craic, colourful hats and clamour,
and someone singing The Fields of Athenry.
We have come a long way.

Garden of Remembrance, Falls Road
for Jinky

Sunlit names on black marble, gold:
volunteers O'Carroll, McCartney, McKelvey, Malone,
ghost me to Columba High woodwork desks –
the last Monday in January nineteen seventy-two –
rain-blurred windows and the room filling
with the steam of youth. Our famine-stained accents
blethering of Buckfast and girls till Duffy howled:
Did yous cunts not see what happened in Derry?

Thirteen dead. Fuckin Brits done it!
And Duffy summoned up ancestral wrath.
Boys! Boys! Register! Our Irish names rung
like bells – over black rosaries for Bloody Sunday –
*Ahearn! Here sir. Breen! Here sir. Callaghan!
Here sir. Duffy!*
There sir.
Pardon?
There, sir.

Outside Of Kilmainham

I count the living beads of a holy rosary
down the strands of my DNA,
The sorrowful mystery of Newgrange, Tara and
Patrick.
Plantation, potatoes, sharks in the coffin ship's wake.
Liberty. Rising. James Connolly tied to a chair.
Sinn Fein rebels whispering partition. Civil War.
Celtic '67. First communion. Bernadette Devlin.
Bloody Sunday, Provos, Brits, Thatcher, Brighton.

I've been tied by rosary beads to a chair.
Destined to be boxer, poet, sinner, raconteur.
Down the gun barrel of time, over seven seas
Famine voices sing *Ave, Ave, Ave Maria.*
A great crowd has choked in my chest.
I gasp, *God's curse on you England you beast.*

How to spell Nationalist

How to spell Nationalist
N is for none shall hunger
in spirit or body or mind.
A is for apple of my eye,
every creed and colour and none because
T is for Thomson,
we're all his daughters and his sons, or the
I that's in between.
O is oidhche mhath
that great sweet Gaelic good night,
and here's another
N for none shall live in fright.
A is for the arrows of your talent,
may they cross like Christmas
comets in the night,
lighting the way homeward for the
L, the lonely of this earth,
the dispossessed. Come away in,
you're in your mammy's,
sit on yer erse, because I is for
I'll stick the kettle oan.
S is for Scotland of course. And?
T? To be continued and improved
by souls as yet unborn.

The Tory

Rain on my skin,
that's what you are.
Snow in my boots.
The wet vest on my back is you.
You untied lace.
You brain freeze.
You faithless fuck.
My wet pocket is you.
My empty purse and
frozen hands.
My unfulfilled destiny.
My dreams are rainbows on the road.
You roadblock, you wall, you chasm,
you downright greedy cunt.
You have worshiped
all the useless Gods
and elbowed to the front.

On est tous des sauvages

At Ted Hughes' house,
a fly-pocked spider's hammock
on hand-shifted, back-breaking stone.
The smokeless chimney
of an old mill waits for lightening
to finish what Thatcher started.
Chainsaws cough out warnings.
The sun pours down the hillside, scorching.
A tree creeper panics up the bark
of the last tree standing.
AW, who was here with a knife
and a sense of the future,
carved into trees
what Hughes carved into paper:
WE ARE ALL SAVAGES.

Fuadach nan Gàidheal
for Andrew Wilson

Sitka spruce thicken yearly, stealing space,
making prisoners of silences. Treetops
tipping less sky into fire roads' whispering
caverns. Sheep tracks tangle the moor like some
ghostly satnav of the fleeing chaos
from homes to the smack of Atlantic sails.
Sheep farms, dams and pylons pollute our dreams
of children lost in dark distracted streams.

Sitka branches knit. Light of foot and flight
sit tight within this fading light, waiting.
This man will find the ragged edge of truth.
He will walk till the trail is lost or gone.
He will dance on the backbone of perdition.
He will close his eyes and sing our songs.

Arc de Triomphe

Traffic lights, lines and rules and lanes and cops
are non-existent so that the perfect
freedom of chaos reigns in swerves and lights
and blaring horns through this steel whirlpool
and suddenly, Delacroix's Liberty
Leading The People strides, making straight for
fleeing tourists. See the comfortably smug –
their mouths wide, lips dripping cake and coffee.

But I, being poor, note her part-bared breasts
smeared with bitter labour. Tricolour wavers
overhead, feet firm on the Champs-Elysées,
coming in Triumph – to free us from these
comfortable shackles – to an economics
feeding the furnace just to keep it lit.

American sweetheart

Nothing's moving in the dawn's early light
except that grey wolf on the tracks. Utah
trains hurtle cold from night frosting the dawn.
Day and dollar rise. Lust is a machine;
she feeds on flesh. Trickles of nickels and dimes
and quarters flow where the hoard of gold ties
yellow ribbon bows on skeletons of dreams
bleaching in the deserts of Afghanistan.

Howling into her thirty-seventh year,
hammering the Arizona blacktop
in his red corvette with the chromium grin,
perfume, leather hide. America's bride
is single now, deceived and sacrificed
by the shimmering eye in the greenback.

Gordonstoun School

Dr Kurt Hahn created this, after Hitler's rise,
to build an upper class with compassionate ways.
A ringing bell – junior prep is over.
A silence, a rummaging, the round square erupts.
At ham and eggs, blue rows of pullovers
hover over rattling plates, consuming.
Every table an odds-on bet as to who will run
the future – this cool boy or that assured girl

dizzy with privilege, back straight, holds stare –
till I look elsewhere. In the chapel following prayer
(or is it a lecture?) it's announced Barnaby Brown's
bag is missing. And it's as serious as that stabbing
in the lane by Dundyvan steelworks in the town
where I was recklessly built by ordinary men.

Body politic

Nicola crosses her legs, looks again at her shoes.
McGowan swore she had braw ankles. Even though
I'm no ankle man I see their merit,
swung there in sling-back high heels.
McGowan, astute for once,
about the foot of the head
of government.
In the unguarded moment of checking
out her shoes, and that slight swing of her leg,
I see a leader whose heels might click and clack

and wobble slightly on a Friday nightly bash,
laughing home with the girls from the pub.
Twelve thousand cheers in this packed-out hall
say Socialism is a shiny new thing stepping away
from the oil and rust and dimly lit rooms
of the broken past. Put on your heels Scotland.
Let's dance.

Uprising

Other cultures – though they bring no soldiers –
still stuff gunpowder in my mouth,
bullets in my nose and ears and their tomorrow
on my eyes and numb my skin with guilt.
But the old ways are in me still, resisting
the colonisation of my soul. Mark my words,
The Troubles have not breathed their last with you.
We won't bring armoured cars nor tanks nor guns.

We will be as shoals of fish or birds of the air,
joyful in our medium, carefree in direction,
wheeling and revolving,
gathering, gathering, gathering.
In splinters of light we will shift, disperse
and be teeming over and around and through
all of history, lighting your deeds as we go.

Shipping

Snug, I lie in night listening to the shipping
forecast bolting the doors of fortress Britain.
South Utsire rising to Gale Force nightmare,
nightwear, sleigh wear, blizzard over Finisterre.
Rockall me off to sleep deep low Hebrides.
Sleet and snow, nowhere to go except slide
down the voice of the night announcer
and cast away the ropes of wakefulness

one by one so that, by his words, my bed floats
in the hiss and boom of a terrible sea
where refugees hang on for morning,
over a cascading fall to their peril,
praying for light and gulls flying over
Malin in a welcome racket of white.

How to spell Ned

N is for not.
It does
Not
mean
Non educated delinquent
Ya spunk trumpet wank truffle cunt fluff.
It's a backronym.
Wanny yous
freckled bespectacled high falutin
nose tilting book munching posh cunts
made it up.
Make ye feel smart did it?
Ya rocket.
Ya fuckin lava lamp.
And E is for Everycunt knows
what yees are upti
cos how can anycunt feel superior
if ye canny look down on other cunts?
Ya fuckin smelly clown's shoe.
Honk honk.
You're trying to keep us D
for down
But know what, Elvis's Y fronts?
ma mind's a super fuckin nova.

A quantum explication of information
multiplied by the speed of light
an all the while yours
is locked in, dubbed up
in what do ye Mc fuckin call it ...
Academia,
slowing yees down
to the speed of the shite
ae Wittgenstein's fly,
stuck tae fuck
in the neck ae the Buckie bottle
I just flung tae fuck.

Publication credits and poem notes

'Daily bread' was published online in Every Day Poets in 2015.

'David's wake' was published in *Poetry Scotland* in 2014.

'Aurora' was published online in Every Day Poets in 2015.

'Dunoon ferry' was published in *The Linnet's Wings* in 2015.

'Five a.m.' was published online in youronephonecall in June/July 2015 and Stares Nest on 8th April 2015.

'The suicide of Michelangelo Prufrock' was published in Poetry Scotland in 2016.

'The rescue dog' was published online in Every Day Poets in 2016.

'McGonnigle hates crows' was published online in youronephonecall on June 21st and July 5th, 2015.

'Never gonna dance' refers to Sean-nós dance – an older style of traditional solo Irish dance. It is a casual dance form, as opposed to the more formal competition-oriented form, of Irish stepdance.

'Survivor' was published online in Every Day Poets in 2016.

'Fuadach nan Gàidheal' is dedicated to Anndra Wilson: Neach-leasachaidh na Gàidhlig.

'Arc de Triomphe' was published in Poetry Scotland in 2014.

'Shipping' was published in *The Linnet's Wings* in 2015.